OBJECT LESSONS
FOR
SPECIAL DAYS

SHERYL BRUINSMA

BAKER BOOK HOUSE

Grand Rapids, Michigan 49506

Copyright 1986 by
Baker Book House Company

ISBN: 0-8010-0920-0

Sixth printing, May 1992

Printed in the United States of America

Contents

New Year

Epiphany

Lent

Palm Sunday

Good Friday

Easter

Ascension Day

Pentecost

Seasons

Mother's Day

Father's Day

Graduation

Using Objects to Teach

Do you want to say something in a way that captures children's attention, drives home your point, and uses a multisensory approach? Use objects!

Jesus used objects to help people understand difficult concepts. Parables are concise and effective ways to make a point. Drawing a parallel with a known or familiar object helps us understand a less tangible one.

This book is intended to give a fresh look at some of our traditional symbols, enlarging meaning and calling attention to the spiritual importance of special days.

The lessons in this book are appropriate for all ages. Young children, however, need a simple vocabulary, a single point, and much repetition. Allow for the needs of the children you address.

An outline is given for each lesson. This helps in skimming for the right material to fit your needs. It also aids in preparing to give the object lesson. I try to give lessons without the use of notes, but I like to have an outline handy. Each outline contains a way to get smoothly in and out of a presentation by making use of the old adages *off to a good start* and *all's well that ends well*. A complete section on how to give an effective object lesson is included in my first book, *New Object Lessons for Children of All Ages* (Baker, 1980). More ideas for lessons can be found in my second book, *Easy-to-Use Object Lessons* (Baker, 1983).

The object lessons in this book have been arranged in the order of a school year. The book is specifically structured to offer help for those special days when you find yourself in need of an effective lesson. It is also useful as devotional material to be read and enjoyed.

Many of the lessons in this book can be used without reference to a special day—just present the concepts they illustrate.

Go ahead and try using objects to teach. It's fun!

1

Everybody Pull Together

(New Season)

Object: A canoe paddle or a drawing of one

Lesson: We all need to accept our responsibilities and work together in order to accomplish our Christian goals.

Text: Whatever you do, work at it with all your heart, as though you were working for God and not for men. [Col. 3:23]

Outline

Introduce object: This paddle reminds me of a canoe trip we took recently.

1. To go straight we need to work together to coordinate our efforts.

2. Go God's way, with the current and not against it.

3. Everybody help.

Conclusion: Let's all use our paddles and with God's help head for a great new season together.

This paddle reminds me of a canoe trip we took recently. The day was sunny, the river was full and moving rapidly, and we were eager to get going. As soon as the canoe was pushed off, I began to paddle as fast as I could. I could hardly believe it when the canoe began to go in circles! The harder I paddled, the faster the canoe turned around and the worse off I was. I learned that to go straight I had to coordinate my efforts with those of the other people in the canoe. We needed equal force on both sides of the canoe. When we worked together, the canoe pulled smoothly ahead.

Let's imagine that our group that's beginning a new season today is in a canoe. To go forward, to reach a goal, to accomplish our purposes we need to coordinate our efforts. We need to work together and exert equal force.

As I mentioned, when we took our canoe trip the river was moving rapidly. Going with the current made our work quite easy. However, at one point we decided to go back and look at something. We soon found that going back, paddling against the current, was exhausting. After making very little progress, we decided that there was no going back for us.

So too in our group we will not look back. We will seek God's purpose and direction for us and "go with the current." The easiest, fastest way to reach our goal is to go God's way and with his help.

After a couple of hours of paddling the canoe, I was really tired. I rested for a few minutes while the others continued to paddle. When I stopped, the others had to work harder and we didn't go as far.

Everybody in our group also needs to do his or her share, work together, accept responsibilities, and pull his or her weight.

Let's all use our paddles and with God's help head for a great new season together.

2

McDonald's Around the World

(Worldwide Communion)

Object: A cup or packaging with McDonald's logo (symbol)

Lesson: Knowing that Christians all over the world celebrate communion makes our world smaller. Our God is the God of the world.

Text: "Do this in memory of me." [1 Cor. 11:24b; read 1 Cor. 11:23–26]

Outline

Introduce object: When we were in Europe this summer with Sarah and Peter, we ate at several McDonald's restaurants.

1. In cities around the world, people are drinking from cups like this one and eating hamburgers.
2. All around the world people are drinking from communion cups, breaking bread, and worshiping God together.

Conclusion: "It's a small world after all."

When we were in Europe this summer with Sarah and Peter, we ate at several McDonald's restaurants. When you travel with eleven- and fourteen-year-olds, you need familiar food at a predictable price. The people in McDonald's in Holland, Germany, and France were drinking out of cups just like this one that I got from our neighborhood McDonald's.

When I look at this cup I am reminded that people all over the world are eating and drinking the same kind of food that we can get. Coke and hamburgers taste pretty much the same wherever you are. I can feel a oneness with people around the world when I think of us all enjoying the same food. I feel that I can share an experience with them.

People around the world are sharing another, far more significant experience today. This is Worldwide Communion Sunday. People from many different lands and cultures are breaking bread, drinking wine, and remembering that Jesus died for them (not just us). God's children come in many colors and speak different languages, but today they are all doing the same thing—worshiping God in the same way. Today we join with people around the world to love God, remember what Jesus did for us, share his spirit, and promise to serve him.

Taking time to think about this makes the world seem smaller and less different. God loves us all and we all love him. "It's a small world after all."

3

Signs the Same in Any Nation

(Worldwide Communion)

Objects: A dirty mirror, window cleaner, and a cloth, or a tarnished object, silver polish, and a cloth

Lesson: We can experience a oneness with all of God's people.

Text: For the bread that God gives is he who comes down from heaven and gives life to the world. [John 6:33]

Outline

Introduce objects: These are symbols which you find all over the world.

1. The pictures or symbols have the same meaning in any nation. The meaning of communion is also the same in any land.

2. The symbols have a deeper meaning. Communion also has a deeper meaning.

Conclusion: This is a special day for remembering and sharing with the world.

These are symbols which you find all over the world. The cigarette in a circle with a line drawn through it means "no smoking." You will find it wherever people are not allowed to smoke. Have you seen these symbols for boys and girls before? Yes, you find them on restroom doors. They give the same message to anyone, even someone who cannot read. It does make life easier to have them. It makes traveling in other countries much easier!

The symbols all have a deeper meaning. The "no smoking" picture can be found in rooms or on trains. It doesn't just mean that you are asked not to smoke. It means that if you do smoke there, someone is very likely to take action against you.

You know that this sign for the girls' room is more than just a label on a door. You know what will happen if you walk into the wrong room. The older you get, the more important these signs become!

The taking of communion is a symbol that God has given to the world. The wine and the bread remind us of Jesus' spilled blood and broken body. You would recognize the taking of communion in a home or church anywhere in the world. You wouldn't need to speak the language. Communion is a symbol we all share. On this Worldwide Communion Sunday we share it at the same time and think about the fact that we are sharing it.

Communion has a deeper meaning as well. It reminds us of more than a broken body and spilled blood. It means that Jesus died for me, for us; that we are clean and free and new in God's sight. It changes our lives.

This is a wonderful day. This is a special day for remembering and sharing with the world.

4

Ever Reforming

(Reformation)

Objects: A dirty mirror, window cleaner, and a cloth, or a tarnished object, silver polish, and a cloth

Lesson: We need to keep our vision of God clear and our faith strong.

Text: Create a pure heart in me, O God,
            and put a new and loyal spirit in me.
                [Ps. 51:10]

Outline

Introduce object: The word *reformation* means a change for the better, an improvement. This mirror certainly needs improvement.

1. Just as this mirror becomes clouded with use, so our beliefs become clouded with the distractions of daily living.

2. This mirror needs to be cleaned and returned to its original condition to be of use. Our faith needs renewing, refining, restoring.

Conclusion: When you are a clean and shining mirror, you can be of use to those around you.

The word *reformation* means a change for the better, an improvement. This mirror certainly needs improvement. I can hardly see myself in it. Fortunately, I don't have to use a mirror that gets dirtier almost every time I try to use it. No, I don't have to throw it away. It is still a good mirror. It just needs a little cleaning. I'll use this window cleaner and a soft cloth.

Our faith and the specific things we believe about God can become cloudy also. We get confused by what we see and hear from those around us. We don't take time to think about what we believe and why. We get used to things that we should question.

The "window cleaner" that brightens, renews, and restores our faith is the Bible. We need to study it and let it speak to our hearts. We need to think about how God's love and concern for us and others should be reflected in our lives. Then we need to live the Christian life in a way which shows that we have a clear, clean understanding of our God, our principles, and our practical beliefs. When you are a clean and shining mirror, you can be of use to those around you.

5

Thanksgiving Is Thanks-Living

(Thanksgiving)

Objects: Two identical small balloons and one large paper bag. Inflate one of the balloons and place it in the bag so that the bag partially collapses and appears to be empty.

Lesson: Being thankful is a frame of mind and a way of life.

Text: . . . be thankful in all circumstances. This is what God wants from you in your life in union with Christ Jesus. [1 Thess. 5:18]

Outline

Introduce object: I have a small balloon with me today.

1. To blow up this little balloon takes a lot of effort. People worry and fret their way through life and use a lot of effort.

2. There is an easier way. People can trust God and live a life of thankfulness.

   a. When you look for ways to be thankful, you find them.

   b. When you are thankful all the time, your life is happier.

3. The balloon was in the bag all along. I just needed to take it. Thankfulness is a way of life that we can take.

Conclusion: Make thanksgiving something you do all the time.

I have a small balloon with me today. I hope I can blow it up for you. It takes a lot of effort to blow this up. (Struggling to inflate the balloon is easy for me. I usually turn red, then blue, from the effort.) I know a lot of people who worry and fret their way through life. They are constantly straining and struggling.

There is an easier way for me to get this balloon blown up. (Drop the balloon into the bag, blow into the bag, then reach in and produce the balloon that is already inflated.) There is also an easier way for people to live. They can trust God to take care of them. Then all they need to do is to relax and thank God. There are extra benefits for people who do this. When you are aware of and looking for good things in your life, you find them. It is similar to the fact that once you have had an illness, you learn of many others who have had it also; once you buy a red car, you notice all of the others of that color. When you begin to look for ways to be thankful, you find more and more of them. When you begin to thank God for all the good things in your life, you become happier. Soon you can be thankful for everything in your life because you see it as part of God's plan for you.

The blown-up balloon was in the bag all the time. I just needed to reach in and take it out. Thankfulness is a way of life—a rejoicing, happy, contented way available for everybody. Just take it. Reach out for a joyful, happy, thankful way of life. Make thanksgiving something you do all of the time.

6

Give Thanks Even for Little Things

(Thanksgiving)

Objects: Key, nail, match, battery, wedding ring

Lesson: We often miss the "little" things in life when we give thanks.

Text: In the name of our Lord Jesus Christ, always give thanks for everything to God the Father. [Eph. 5:20]

Outline

Introduce objects: We have many obvious things for which we are thankful: food, shelter, family, jobs. It is easy to remember the big things. I have some little things with me today to help us remember more.

1. Key—a bit of truth that unlocks a mystery or solves a problem
2. Nail—kindness, which holds people together
3. Match—enthusiasm
4. Battery—energy
5. Wedding ring—symbol

Conclusion: We have so much for which to give thanks. Look for the little things, which just might turn out to be the biggest things of all.

We have many obvious things for which we are thankful: food, shelter, family, jobs. It is easy to remember the big things. I have some little things with me today to help us remember more.

The first item is a key. Without a key you could be locked out of your house. Or you couldn't get into a jewelry box, a diary, or a special drawer. A "key" in our lives for which we might be thankful might be a bit of truth that unlocks a mystery, knowledge that solves a problem, or wisdom to deal with a situation.

This little nail can join two pieces of wood permanently. It can fix a broken object or hang a picture. The "nail" in our lives is the kindness that can bond people together. It is the understanding that mends a broken relationship.

Here is a match. A camping trip would be a disaster without one. In my case a camping trip needs a book or two of matches! This match represents enthusiasm for God's cause, a spark of faith to pass around, the warmth of support for God's people.

A battery is stored energy. Energy is important for following through on projects, carrying out our responsibilities, living an effective Christian life. God gives us this energy so we can spread his love.

This wedding ring symbolizes marriage. In a similar way, we have symbols of our faith. We can be thankful, for God gives us these reminders to make our beliefs more real and clear in our lives. They are little things that enrich and bring deeper meaning to our lives.

We have so much for which to give thanks. Look for the little things, which just might turn out to be the biggest things of all.

7

A Song of Thanksgiving

(Thanksgiving)

Objects: Something to write words and music on: a chalkboard and chalk or a large piece of paper and markers

Lesson: Singing is one way to express our thanks to God.

Text: Let us come before him with thanksgiving and sing joyful songs of praise. [Ps. 95:2]

Outline

Introduction: God wants us to thank him. One good way to thank, praise, and love him is to make our own song to sing.

1. Sing the song. Use the children's names or your own.
2. Have as many children as possible mention something for which they are thankful. Add these to the words of the middle line of music. Repeat the line as often as necessary. Sing the song each time a line has been added or wait until two or more have volunteered if there are many children. The completed song will be one of thanks and praise from all of the children, both singly and collectively.

Conclusion: A prayer of love and commitment

God wants us to thank him. One good way to thank, praise, and love him is to make our own song to sing. This is a song of thanksgiving. (Follow instructions in point 2 of the outline.)

We thank you, heav'n-ly Fa - ther, for man - y things.

_____ thanks you for her _____. _____thanks you for his _____.

We thank you, heav'n - ly Fa - ther, for all these things.

Prayer: God our Father, we all do thank you—each of us from his or her heart—for the things we sang about in our song. Accept our praise and thanks. Help us to live thankful lives. Amen.

8

An Advent Chain

(An Advent Activity)

The purpose of an Advent chain is to give children a meaningful way to count the days until Christmas.

Making an Advent Chain

The only materials needed to make an Advent chain are the links. You will need one link for every day until Christmas (twenty-five links, if the chain is constructed on or before December 1). Links of the chain are made from strips of construction paper. The links can be of various colors of paper (you may wish to use a special color for Christmas Day).

Print a message or an attribute on each link. Older children can do this for themselves or for younger children. Or use a ditto machine to make copies of the messages on the links before you cut them. If you do this, number the messages so the colors can be varied and the links sorted later with one of each message for each Advent chain.

If you choose to make an attribute chain, print twenty-five Christian characteristics on the links of the chain: hope, love, peace, faith, kindness, thankfulness, generosity, faithfulness, trust, obedience, reverence, meekness, humility, long-suffering, patience, sympathy, thoughtfulness, loyalty, sweetness, purity, charity, simplicity, beauty, enthusiasm, joy.

Another alternative—especially useful for a group—is to list twenty-five activities. These activities can include reading passages of Scripture, praying about special concerns, bringing gifts or otherwise expressing love for the sick and shut-ins, communicating with someone special to the children, or making or doing something for a loved one.

An Advent chain that is used in a Sunday-school room can contain five special messages—one for each week of Advent and one for Christmas.

Glue or staple the links together to form a chain. Hang the chain from a cardboard or stiff paper shape, such as a star.

Using an Advent Chain

Cut or gently tear off a link each day. Read the message and discuss with the child how he can act on the message or show the attribute in his life. The chain provides a way for the child and his family to focus on the significance of Advent.

9

An Advent Wreath

(Advent)

Object: An Advent wreath (an evergreen wreath with four candles placed in it [purple, blue, or white and pink—different traditions use different colors] and a larger candle in the center)

Lesson: The Advent wreath is a symbol of our preparation for Christmas.

Text: "She will have a son, and you will name him Jesus—because he will save his people from their sins." [Matt. 1:21]

Outline

Introduce object: The Advent wreath is a symbol of our faith.

1. An unending circle of love and friendship is represented by the circle of the wreath.

2. The evergreen stands for our constant and lasting commitment.

3. The candles represent Jesus as the light of the world and our act of giving of ourselves.

Conclusion: When we light our Advent candles let us think of all that this symbol of our faith has to say to us.

The Advent wreath is a symbol of our faith. That means it stands for and reminds us of some important truths or Christian beliefs. It also helps us prepare our hearts for the important day to come this month—Christmas. The wreath is used by lighting a candle each Sunday. Each candle has a special meaning. The last, largest, and center candle is lighted on Christmas Eve or Christmas Day.

Let's take a look at the wreath itself. It is a circle. A circle has no beginning and no end. It represents our love for God and his people and our friendship with each other. This love and friendship never ends but keeps going (gesture around and around the wreath).

An Advent wreath is made from evergreen branches. Evergreen trees do not shed their leaves in the fall. They are never bare. This represents our commitment to Christ, which is constant—it goes forever. It does not become dormant during certain times of the year, but is constantly alive.

The center candle stands for Jesus, who is the light of the world. We light it on Christmas when we remember his light coming into our world. The other candles remind us that in order for us to shine for Jesus, we need to give of ourselves.

When we light our Advent candles let us think of all that this symbol of our faith has to say to us.

Using an Advent Wreath

Each time a candle is lighted, a short message is read to remind the people of the symbolism.

First candle: We celebrate the coming of Jesus' birthday because he is the **hope** of the world. Sing "Come, Thou Long-Expected Jesus."

Second candle: We celebrate the coming of Jesus' birthday

because he is the center of our **faith.** Sing "O Come, O Come, Emmanuel."

Third candle: We celebrate the coming of Jesus' birthday because it shows us how much God **loves** us. Sing "O Come, All Ye Faithful."

Fourth candle: We are **joyful** because the birthday of Jesus is almost here. Sing "Joy to the World."

Center candle: We celebrate the birth of a small child and the angels' message: "Glory to God in the highest and on earth **peace,** good will to men." Sing "Silent Night."

10
An Advent List

(Advent)

Object: A Christmas list. I cut two pieces of paper length-wise and glued them together to make a very long, half-sized sheet.

Lesson: Prepare your heart for the celebration of Christmas.

Text: Mary said,
     "My heart praises the Lord;
       my soul is glad because of God my Savior,
       for he has remembered me, his lowly servant!
     From now on all people will call me happy."
         [Luke 1:46–48]

Outline

Introduce object: In this Advent season we make preparations for Christmas. This is my list.

1. The importance of preparation
2. The joy of anticipation

Conclusion: Jesus' birthday is coming. Let's get ready!

In this Advent season we make preparations for Christmas. This is my list (unroll a long, long list). When I was your age, the list of what I wanted for Christmas was this long. Now the list of things I need to do and want to buy is this long. It took me a lot of time to write this list and I would be lost without it. On my list in big letters is the most important thing I need to do—prepare my thoughts and heart for celebrating Jesus' birthday. When you make your list of things you really need for Christmas, don't forget to include a loving, happy, thankful heart. Remember that the reason we give gifts is because Christmas is a party for Jesus' birthday.

The hardest part of buying just the right gift for someone is waiting until Christmas to give it to him or her. That anticipation is also part of the fun. The joyful anticipation of the celebration of Jesus' birthday is a big part of Christmas. I can't wait to share the fun and the love and the warmth of this wonderful season.

Jesus' birthday is coming. Let's get ready!

11

A Closer Look

(Advent)

Object: Binoculars

Lesson: Take a closer look at what Christmas means to you.

Text: "And he will be called 'Immanuel' (which means, 'God is with us')." [Matt. 1:23b]

Outline

Introduce object: Have you ever looked through a pair of binoculars?

1. Binoculars make things look closer. Take a closer look at Christmas.

2. Looking through the wrong end of binoculars makes things seem to be farther away. Mention things that make Christmas appear further away, less meaningful.

Conclusion: Now is the time to stop and put things in proper perspective. You must decide what Christmas means to you!

Have you ever looked through a pair of binoculars? They are great when you want to take a closer look at something that is far away. They make people who are not too far away from me look like I can touch them. You look close!

I brought the binoculars with me today because I want to talk about taking a closer look at something that happened a long time ago. That event can have a powerful effect on your life. During the Advent season we prepare our hearts and minds to celebrate the birth of Jesus. As Christmas approaches it is appropriate to think of the true meaning of Christmas—not the gifts and goodies but the coming of Jesus to earth. What does this mean in your life? Does the fact that Jesus came to earth almost two thousand years ago make a difference to you personally? Would your life be different without his advent? Is Christmas a time of special meaning for you?

If you look into the wrong end of binoculars, things look very far away. Often, without even realizing it, we are looking into the wrong end of Christmas. The true meaning seems very far away. How do we make the true meaning of Christmas harder to reach? Often we make ourselves too busy, too tired, too preoccupied, too self-centered, too demanding, or too interested in getting the perfect gifts.

When you pick up binoculars you need to make sure you have the right end toward your eyes. Advent is the season to make sure you are looking at the right end of Christmas. Now is the time to stop and put things in proper perspective. You must decide what Christmas means to you!

12

A Musical Card

(Christmas)

Object: A musical Christmas card

Lesson: The joy of the Christmas season comes from within.

Text: Restore unto me the joy of thy salvation; and uphold me with thy free spirit. [Ps. 51:12, KJV]

Outline

Introduce object: The new musical Christmas cards are a lot of fun.

1. Music comes from within.

2. The card plays music only when it is opened.

3. Music represents the joy that is central to the Christmas season.

Conclusion: Like the music from this card, let the joy of this blessed season come from deep within you and reach out to all of those around you at this very special time of year.

The new musical Christmas cards are a lot of fun. I enjoy sneaking up on them and popping them open and shut. I like the music they play and trying to figure out how they do it. Listen to this card.

When I first saw these cards I found it hard to believe that music could come from inside of a nearly flat card. However, music *does* come from inside of it. Music comes from inside of *us* as well. It is an expression of our inner selves. It is a form of worship.

This card won't play unless it is opened. When I close it, the music stops immediately. Have you ever tried to sing when you are "shut up"—unhappy, angry with someone, depressed, or not feeling well? In order to sing, you need to feel that you can open up to the world around you; that you can reach out to the love and fellowship of others; that you can share the happiness in your soul. The best thing about singing is that even when you don't feel these things when you start, this giving of yourself can make you happier.

This card represents the joy of the season because it "sings." Singing is a natural expression of the joy that is central to this Christmas season. We have many wonderful songs to sing about Jesus' birth, praising God and asking for a meaningful time of commitment.

Like the music from this card, let the joy of this blessed season come from deep within you and reach out to all of those around you at this very special time of year.

13

You Can't Judge a Package by Its Wrapping

(Christmas)

Objects: Two wrapped gifts, a plain one containing a nice gift and a fancy one containing something of little value

Lesson: It is what is inside that counts.

Text: But the LORD said unto him, "Pay no attention to how tall and handsome he is. I have rejected him, because I do not judge as man judges. Man looks at the outward appearance, but I look at the heart." [1 Sam. 16:7]

Outline

Introduce objects: Which of these two presents would you rather have?

1. You can't choose a present by its wrapping. You can't judge people by their appearance.
2. You find out what's in a package by unwrapping it. You must take the time and make the effort to get to know people.

Conclusion: I don't like to choose a package by its wrapping. I'm glad I don't have to choose friends that way.

Which of these two presents would you rather have? The fancy one is prettier. It is larger too. This other one does have something inside of it. It could be better. Which one should I open?

Like packages, people come in all sizes and colors. Some have more attractive wrappings than others. How can you find out which one would make the best friend?

You want me to open this fancy package? There is something in here someplace; I can hear it rattle. Here it is—a pencil. I guess anyone can always use an extra pencil. What do you think is in this other package? An eraser? Let's see. A gold ring! Now that is something really special. It will increase in value the longer it is kept.

It is not quite as easy to find out what is inside of people. It takes more time and energy than the simple unwrapping I just did. What did Jesus do when he lived on earth? What example did he set for us? He spent time with many different kinds of people. He talked to them. He helped them. When you are willing to do this, you discover the uniqueness of each person. You may find a friendship more valuable than a gold ring—one that increases in value as you keep it.

Giving of yourself to others not only enriches your life but also can make a big difference in the life of someone else. A lonely, sad person will light up when you give him or her a smile. An older person may have many fascinating stories to share. A sick person will feel better because you have taken the time to care. A positive comment warms the heart of anyone!

I don't like to choose a package by its wrapping. I'm glad I don't have to choose friends that way.

14
Colored Lights
(Christmas)

Object: A string of colored lights

Lesson: Let everyone shine from within and be part of the Christmas season.

Text: "In the same way your light must shine before people, so that they will see the good things you do and praise your Father in heaven." [Matt. 5:16]

Outline

Introduce object: One of the things I like best about Christmas is the strings of colored lights found on trees, around windows, and across roofs.

1. Light shines out from the bulbs. The Christmas spirit comes from within us and shines out for all to see.

2. Lights must be connected to an electrical outlet. Christians must be plugged in to the love of God.

3. Every bulb must be connected. Every person must participate.

4. People and bulbs come in all colors.

5. Colored lights represent a celebration. Christmas is a celebration.

Conclusion: Are you plugged in and shining for Jesus today?

One of the things I like best about Christmas is the strings of colored lights found on Christmas trees, around windows, and across roofs. They remind me of so many things.

Each bulb has a filament in the center which produces light to shine out for everyone to see. There is a special Christmas spirit that comes from within each Christian and shines out to everyone around us as well.

These lights can shine only when they are hooked up to the power source. You can't put strings of lights up where the cord can't somehow be connected to an electrical outlet. Christians need to be plugged in to the love of God. His love is the power source for the unique glow of anticipation that is part of the Christian spirit.

If you remove one of these bulbs, they will all go out. Christians also need to work together. The Christmas season is one of friendship and sharing. Each member is important to the group. Each one is necessary. One person copping out, turning away, or pulling loose affects everyone.

These bulbs are all the same on the inside, but the glass is painted or stained different colors. People come in different colors too, but they are alike on the inside. Different colors make the lights and people more interesting. These colored lights represent a celebration. So too we are all celebrating an important event in Christian tradition. The birth of Jesus is a very special time. Join in the festivities! Are you plugged in and shining for Jesus today?

15

Peace on Earth

(Christmas)

Object: A large balloon (blow it up halfway). Place a piece of plastic tape on the balloon. Pins can be inserted into the balloon through the tape without popping the balloon.

Lesson: Peace comes by spreading the love of God.

Text: "Glory to God in the highest, and on earth peace, good will toward men." [Luke 2:14, KJV]

Outline

Introduce object: What will happen if I stick a pin into this balloon?

1. How can you keep a balloon from popping? How can you keep peace in a potentially explosive world?

2. Plastic tape keeps the pins from popping the balloon. The special holding power of God's love holds the world together.

3. Pass on this secret. Peace starts with you and is spread to others.

Conclusion: Let this Christmas season be the beginning of peace on earth, good will toward men.

What will happen if I stick a pin into this balloon? Would you like me to do it? I'll be careful; I don't like sudden, loud noises. Ah, it's in and the balloon didn't pop. Can you believe your eyes and your ears?

How can you keep a balloon from popping when you stick a pin into it? It seems impossible—just like asking how you can keep peace in a potentially explosive world.

I'll tell you the secret and you can pass it on. You blow up the balloon about halfway. Then you put a piece of plastic tape on the balloon. When you carefully put pins into the tape, the balloon doesn't break. Look, I'll do it again. Now, what can help us hold this world together? I can think of only one force strong enough for that. The special holding power of God's love is the only thing strong enough for such an enormous task!

What was the message of the angels to the shepherds? It was "glory to God in the highest, and on earth peace, good will toward men." Peace starts with you! You pass it on to others by sharing God's love and loving them. They in turn pass on this special feeling and power to others.

It's your turn to share the message of the angels with those around you, to take the love of God and share his spirit and power in the world. It is a huge task but it must begin somewhere. Let this Christmas season be the beginning of peace on earth, good will toward men.

16

A Christmas Wish

(Christmas)

Object: A gift package with a piece of paper inside. The paper bears the following message: "The person who holds this paper is entitled to one wish, providing he or she does not wish for more wishes."

Lesson: If you had one wish, would it be selfish or selfless?

Text: The LORD is my shepherd;
             I have everything I need. [Ps. 23:1]

Outline

Introduce object: I wonder what is inside of this package.

1. Wish for things.

2. Wish for health, happiness, or wisdom.

3. Wish for others you know.

4. Wish for the world.

Conclusion: God gives me everything I need. I think I'll make a wish for others. What would you do?

I wonder what is inside of this package. Would you like me to open it? There is only a piece of paper in here. Wait, there is something written on it. Let me read it. "The person who holds this paper is entitled to one wish, providing he or she does not wish for more wishes." Well, I can't be too greedy, but what should I wish for? What would you want?

I could wish for a new car or a house or a big boat. I would like any of those things. How about a whole new wardrobe? I could use some new clothes! There are so many things I want that I can't decide. How about you?

Perhaps I should wish for something lasting . . . like good health for the rest of my life. I could wish to always be happy or wise. What do you think about that?

So far I have thought about only myself and what I want. What could I wish for my family, for my friends, for my neighbors, or for my church? I could give happiness to a lot of people. What do you think I should do? What would you do if you were me?

Wait, I could wish for something for the whole world. Do you think that would be a good idea? Would you do that? Just to think about it makes me excited. I could wish that there would be no more hunger. In keeping with the Christmas season, I could wish for peace on earth, good will toward men. It would mean that I would have to give up wishing for something for myself. Would you be willing to do that?

God gives me everything I need. I think I'll make a wish for others. What would you do?

17

Food for Thought

(Christmas)

Object: Replica or drawing of a manger

Lesson: Make the celebration of Christmas simple, humble, and real.

Text: "You will find a baby wrapped in cloths and lying in a manger." [Luke 2:12b]

Outline

Introduce object: Do you know what this is? That's right, it is a manger, a feeding trough for animals. A manger is where Jesus was placed after he was born.

1. A manger is soft, clean, and above the floor.

2. A stable is more private, less crowded, and freer from germs than an inn is.

3. The manger holds food for the animals. It can give us food for thought about the meaning of Christmas.

Conclusion: Let this Christmas be a humble, heartwarming, happy, simple time!

D o you know what this is? That's right, it is a manger, a feeding trough for animals. A manger is where Jesus was placed after he was born. It has clean hay in it and is built so the animals can reach in or pull the hay from between these slats. It keeps the food from being dragged around on the floor.

God could have chosen anywhere for his son to be born and placed. Why did he choose a manger? A manger is soft and clean and above the floor. It was really a good place to put a baby. It was also a simple and natural place.

Why was Jesus born in a stable? Do you think that is a terrible place? Last summer we visited a life-sized inn of that time in a museum. It was built to be like the one in which Joseph and Mary looked for a room. It was safe, but it was crowded, not very clean, busy with people coming and going, noisy with loud laughter and storytelling, and smelling of the sweat and stale food of the travelers. That would have been a poor place for a baby to be born. The stable was private, uncrowded, free from the germs of people with colds, and warm from the sleeping animals. God chose a good place, a safe place, a suitable place. It was a humble and peaceful place—not much like our Christmas places filled with noise, commercialism, commotion, and greediness. Some people set their expectations so high that they can never be fulfilled. Instead, we need to keep the celebration of Christmas simple and fulfilling. Don't want more from Christmas than you should and you will indeed be fulfilled.

Jesus was laid in a place where there was food for animals. Thinking about the circumstances of Jesus' birth can be food for our souls, food for thought. Christmas is a time to remember and believe, a time to listen to the cry of a baby in the night, a time to listen to the small voice of love in our hearts. Let this Christmas be a humble, heartwarming, happy, simple time!

18

A Happy New Year

(New Year)

Object: A snakeskin or a picture of a snakeskin (or a shell that a sea animal has left because it has been outgrown)

Lesson: God has given you a new year for a fresh start. Use it wisely.

Text: This is the new being which God, its Creator, is constantly renewing in his own image, in order to bring you to a full knowledge of himself. [Col. 3:10]

Outline

Introduce object: Do you know what a snake does when its skin gets too tight?

1. A snake outgrows its skin and sheds it. People need a new chance.

2. A snake grows a new skin. Take the new year to renew your hearts and minds.

Conclusion: God is giving you a new year—a fresh start on the rest of your life. Use it wisely!

D o you know what a snake does when its skin gets too tight? It sheds its skin. The skin it crawls out of looks like this.

Now I have to admit that I would rather hold a snake's skin than a live snake. I'm glad that the snake is through with this skin.

Have any of you done anything this year that you wished you had not done? People often need a "fresh skin"—a new start, a chance to feel unburdened by past mistakes. God will give this to us any time we pray for forgiveness, but the new year is a special time at which we say thank you to God for the old year and pray for a new year that will be better.

When the snake sheds its skin, it grows a new one. When we "shed" the old year, we have a new, fresh, promising one ready for us. We have a new year to learn more about God and his greatness. We have a new year to live a more complete Christian life. Think of something you can do to make this year a better one. How can it be more fulfilling than last year? What can you do to avoid the mistakes you made last year? What things can you concentrate on to improve in this new year? When we decide on these things they are called new year's resolutions.

God is giving you a new year—a fresh start on the rest of your life. Use it wisely!

19

A New Notebook

(New Year)

Object: A new spiral notebook

Lesson: Make a commitment to live a constant, dedicated Christian life in this new year.

Text: Your hearts and minds must be made completely new. [Eph. 4:23]

Outline

Introduce object: I have a new notebook. It is clean—no writing in it anywhere.

1. Commitment—a promise to write; a promise to live a more dedicated Christian life
2. Contributions—decide what you will write; decide how you will live this Christian life
3. Constancy—keep it up

Conclusion: This is a new, clean chance for a wonderful Christian year.

I have a new notebook. It is clean—no writing in it any-where. It is just what I need and it will help me tell you the significance we place on a new year as a fresh start, a new year to live a life of Christian dedication.

First, you need commitment. Just as you have to pick up a pen or pencil and decide to write in a new notebook, so too must you decide to make this year count. You make a commitment, a promise, to live a better, fuller, richer Christian life.

Then you need to concentrate on what will be your contributions. What exactly will you write in the new book? What will you do to live a more dedicated Christian life? You need to think of ways to make your Christian commitment count: helping people, meeting the needs of others, spending more time in prayer, learning more about God, working on an area of weakness.

Finally, you need to be constant in your commitment. That means you need to keep it up, to work at it all the time—not start and stop when you please. I'll never get this notebook filled if I forget it and leave it behind when I need it. A new year's resolution will work only if you stay with it. This is a new, clean chance for a wonderful Christian year.

20

What Will You Give Him?

(Epiphany)

Object: A container that resembles one the wise men might have carried

Lesson: Following the wise men's example, what will you give Jesus?

Text: Jesus was born in the town of Bethlehem in Judea, during the time when Herod was king. Soon afterward, some men who studied the stars came from the East to Jerusalem and asked, "Where is the baby born to be the king of the Jews? We saw his star when it came up in the east, and we have come to worship him." [Matt. 2:1–2]

Outline

Introduce object: I chose this container because I thought it looked like something the wise men might have used to carry their gold, frankincense, and myrrh.

1. The wise men gave much. What will you give?

    a. Expensive gifts

    b. Time

    c. Trouble

2. The wise men came to worship Jesus. How will you worship him?

Conclusion: How much are you willing to do for him?

I chose this container because I thought it looked like something the wise men might have used to carry their gold, frankincense, and myrrh. Epiphany is the day set aside to remember the coming of the wise men. We don't know much about them except that they lived in the east and studied the stars. While they were studying they saw a sign in the heavens that meant a king was born to the Jews. They made a long and difficult trip to Jerusalem, where they asked Herod to help them find the baby. Herod's experts said the baby would be in Bethlehem. Herod wanted to find the baby so he could kill him. Herod was the ruler and he didn't want another king. The wise men found the baby but they didn't tell Herod.

We know that the wise men came with expensive gifts to give Jesus. Even if we can't make a trip to see the baby, we can still give Jesus gifts. He said that whatever we give to others in his name is the same as if we give it to him. What will you give him?

The wise men also spent a lot of time in search of Jesus. It took about two years before they found him in a house in Bethlehem. We can also give Jesus time—time to serve him by helping others and time spent with him in prayer and fellowship.

It was difficult and dangerous to travel so far in those days. The wise men were dedicated to the cause of finding Jesus. Jesus is worthy of our time, energy, concern, and dedication. How much trouble are you willing to endure for Jesus?

Why did the wise men come so far? They came to worship Jesus. How far would you go to worship Jesus? How much are you willing to do for him?

21

A Wonderful Trip

(Epiphany)

Object: A balloon which you can blow up until it pops—or have someone else who is willing to do this for you. Tape a thumbtack inside your hand with a bandaid if you wish to control when the balloon pops.

Lesson: Seeking Jesus can be exciting.

Text: And so they left, and on their way they saw the same star they had seen in the East. When they saw it, how happy they were, what joy was theirs! [Matt. 2:9]

Outline

Introduce object: Have you ever blown up a balloon until it pops—on purpose?

1. The wise men's trip and blowing up the balloon share four characteristics.

   a. Takes a lot of nerve

   b. Takes a long time

   c. Filled with uncertainty

   d. Continue in spite of danger

2. The wise men had the satisfaction of having accom-

plished their purpose. We can have that same satisfaction.

Conclusion: It was a wonderful trip!

Have you ever blown up a balloon until it pops—on purpose? Would you like me to do it? Okay, but it takes a lot of nerve. It took a lot of nerve for the wise men to set out on their trip to find the baby who was born to be king of the Jews. The wise men were people who studied the stars and they had seen a special star that meant a king had been born to the Jews. They wanted to find him, even though they knew that it wouldn't be easy.

It is going to take me a long time and a lot of energy to blow up this balloon until it pops. The wise men knew it would take them a long time to find this baby. We think it took about two years. At the rate I'm going with this balloon it might take that long!

The trip of the wise men was filled with uncertainty. Travel was difficult. Instead of cars, they had temperamental camels. There were no good roads. Bandits often attacked travelers. I'm uncertain about when this balloon will pop and what will happen when it does. That uncertainty is an uncomfortable feeling.

When the wise men came to Jerusalem, they had to ask Herod, the Roman ruler, where they could find this baby. Herod didn't want the Jews to have their own king. It was dangerous for the wise men to go and ask him, but they didn't know where to look themselves. Herod's experts looked up the law and found out that the baby would be born in Bethlehem. Herod tried to trick the wise men into finding the baby and coming back and telling him where he was. It was dangerous for them to continue on their quest. Do you want me to continue blowing up this balloon? (If the balloon has not already popped, blow until it does or pop it with the concealed tack.)

The wise men did accomplish their mission. They found the small child in a house and worshiped him. We too can find Jesus and worship him. Then the wise men went back home a different way to keep away from Herod (they had been warned in a dream). It was a wonderful trip!

22

Spring Cleaning

(Lent)

Object: A vacuum, a special cleaning tool, or a collection of cleaning supplies

Lesson: Lent is the time to prepare your hearts to reconsider the impact of Jesus' death on your lives.

Text: "Clean what is inside the cup first, and then the outside will be clean too!" [Matt. 23:26b; read Matt. 23:25–28]

Outline

Introduce object: How many of you have to clean your own bedrooms?

1. Ways to clean a bedroom and your heart:
   a. Surface cleaning—throw things under the bed or in a closet; put off thinking about preparation
   b. More thorough cleaning—pick up belongings and put them away, make bed; put your life in order
   c. Complete cleaning—clean the entire room, including the closets; serious thinking
2. Tools to use when you clean

Conclusion: When your bedroom is clean you feel so good. Try a clean heart and mind!

How many of you have to clean your own bedrooms? I certainly can remember doing it when I was young. Now I have to clean a whole house. These are some of the cleaning supplies I use. They make the job a little easier. Lent is a time of preparing or cleaning your heart so there is room to consider the full meaning of what Jesus did for you so long ago. Lent starts forty weekdays before Easter. Many people spend this time in fasting and prayer.

There are different ways to clean a bedroom. One is to throw everything under the bed, in a closet, or in a toy chest and run outside before you get caught. Some people prepare their hearts for Easter by saying, "That time of year again. I'll give it some thought later."

A better way to clean your room is to pick up your things and put them where they belong and make your bed. A better way to prepare your heart is to put your life in order—decide what things are important and make up your mind to have Christ at the center of it.

The most thorough way to clean your bedroom is to give it a complete or "spring" cleaning. To give your heart a complete cleaning is to think seriously about the sacrifice Jesus made for you and then sacrifice something yourself—something you really like. Clean the closets of your mind by sorting out unnecessary thoughts and replacing them with better ones.

These are the tools I use to clean my house. The tools to clean your heart are prayer, soul-searching, serious thought, quiet love and praise, and taking specific action on something meaningful.

When your bedroom is clean you feel so good. Try a clean heart and mind!

23

It Can't Be Measured

(Lent)

Object: A large, clean container of sugar (or salt or other grained substance)

Lesson: God's love as evidenced by the gift of his Son is too great to be measured or counted.

Text: The LORD is great and is to be highly praised;
         his greatness is beyond understanding.
         [Ps. 145:3]

Outline

Introduce object: How many grains of sugar do you think are in this large jar?

1. Just as you can't count the grains of sugar, you can't count the ways God shows his love.

2. Sugar is measured in another way. You measure God's love by its effect on your life.

3. Sugar is an important ingredient in recipes. God giving his Son is *the* important ingredient in our salvation.

Conclusion: During this season of Lent, think of ways to thank God and show your love for him.

How many grains of sugar do you think are in this large jar? (Show young children some of the grains on your finger or theirs.) Would somebody like to count them? Why not? You're right. It would be an impossible task. God's love is also far too great to be counted. He shows it to us in many, many ways.

When we use sugar, we don't have to count the grains. We have other ways of measuring it. We use it by the spoonful for cereal, coffee, or tea. For recipes we use it by the cup or part of a cup. How do we measure God's love? We don't have any standard measurements to use, but we feel it, we share it, we appreciate it.

Sugar is an important ingredient in many things. Some people may not eat sugar—think how difficult that must be. I can't imagine my favorite dessert without sugar.

I can't imagine this world without the love of God. This season called Lent is when we prepare our hearts to remember and celebrate the biggest example of love that has ever been shown. God gave his own Son to die for our sins so that we might be made whole. Now that is a greater love than could ever be counted or measured. During this season of Lent, think of ways to thank God and show your love for him.

24

Meet My Imaginary Elephant

(Palm Sunday)

Object: Describe an imaginary elephant (this can be a lot of fun to do).

Lesson: Examine what Palm Sunday means to you.

Text: When Jesus entered Jerusalem, the whole city was thrown into an uproar. "Who is he?" the people asked. [Matt. 21:10; read Matt. 21:1–11]

Outline

Introduce object: My object is invisible, but I will describe it.

1. Tell the story of four blind men.

   a. One feels the trunk of an elephant and thinks it is a large snake.

   b. One feels the side and thinks it is a wall.

   c. Another feels the leg and thinks it is a tree.

   d. The last feels the tail and thinks it is a rope.

2. The people present on Palm Sunday reacted differently to what they saw.

   a. Some people saw the royal treatment and welcomed the new king.

b. Some saw the parade and were carried away with the excitement.

c. Others saw a man who was fulfilling prophecy and doing miracles.

d. The Pharisees saw a man they disliked and were upset by the attention he was getting.

Conclusion: What does Palm Sunday mean to you? Do you have the whole picture?

M y object is invisible, but I will describe it. Move over, it is a very big elephant. Watch out! He might step on your toes. His head is over here. Be careful of his trunk. He likes to swing it around and he might grab something of yours. His tail is way over here. He is *this* tall (gesture) with big thick legs and rough, tough skin.

I'm going to tell you an old story of four blind men. They were told that an elephant was nearby. None of them had ever seen one. "I'll go over and feel the elephant and tell you what it is like," volunteered the first blind man. He found his way over to a long, fat, wiggly thing and felt it. Then he returned to the other men and said, "An elephant is like a very large writhing snake. I'm staying away from it."

"That doesn't sound quite right," said another blind man. "I'll have to feel for myself." He went over and felt the tall, rough sides of the elephant. "It feels like a wall to me. Nothing to be afraid of."

The third blind man said, "That doesn't fit with what I've heard of elephants. I'm going to check." He walked over and grabbed hold of one of the elephant's thick legs. He came back to his friends. "I can hardly believe it, but an elephant is like a tree!"

"You must all be wrong," said the fourth blind man. He

went over and felt the elephant's tail. "Now that's strange! An elephant feels very much like a rope."

All of the blind men were right and yet they all were wrong. They did not have the whole picture.

So too there were many opinions about what was happening on Palm Sunday. Some people saw the royal treatment Jesus was receiving. They heard people welcoming him as a king. They were happy about seeing royalty and expecting freedom from Roman rule.

Other people saw the parade and were carried away by the shouting and the waving of palm branches. It was a time for fun and celebrating.

Some people were there because they had heard about the prophecy that Jesus was fulfilling when he rode into Jerusalem on a donkey. They knew about his miracles. They wanted to worship him and show him respect.

The Pharisees saw a man they disliked. He was getting attention and they were upset. "Look at the way the people are treating him! It is disgusting the way he is getting all of that attention! What can we do to stop this?"

All of these people were right according to their own view, but none of them had the whole picture. They knew only part of what was happening. What does Palm Sunday mean to you? Do you have the whole picture?

25

Wave Your Pompons

(Palm Sunday)

Object: Pompons or other articles that cheerleaders use

Lesson: On Palm Sunday we celebrate the triumphant entry of Jesus into Jerusalem. We have reason to rejoice!

Text: When he came near Jerusalem, at the place where the road went down the Mount of Olives, the large crowd of his disciples began to thank God and praise him in loud voices for all the great things that they had seen.
[Luke 19:37]

Outline

Introduce object: I remember going to many basketball games where cheerleaders waved their pompons and shouted cheers.

1. Pompons are a little like palm branches.

2. Their purpose is to raise excitement and cheer people on.

3. The people expected a winner. They got one—but they didn't know it was a different kind of a game.

Conclusion: We *do* know and that gives us even more reason to rejoice. Let's use this day to say, "Hurrah for Jesus!"

I remember going to many basketball games where cheerleaders waved their pompons and shouted cheers (shake pompons while you talk). It made the game more exciting.

Waving these pompons is a modern version of waving palm branches, like the people did long ago for Jesus. When Jesus was riding into Jerusalem the week before he died, a crowd of people waved palm branches and shouted. They were excited about seeing Jesus and welcoming him. This is why we call this day Palm Sunday.

The cheers that the cheerleaders shout at a ball game encourage the players. They also raise excitement in the spectators. This happened on Palm Sunday as people cheered and shouted, "God bless the King of Israel." The people were excited about this king who had come to rescue them from the political rulers of that time.

Those people cheered a winner—and Jesus *was* a winner! But it was a different "game" than the people thought it was. He had come not to save them from the rule of the Romans but to save them from their sins.

Jesus was the winner of a far more important event—he conquered death. The people of that day didn't know how important his task was. We *do* know and that gives us even more reason to rejoice. Let's use this day to say, "Hurrah for Jesus!"

26

Even Better

(Palm Sunday)

Objects: A pitcher of water and a glass with powdered drink mix in it. Use a colored glass or one with a design on it if the children will be close enough to see the powder. Set the glass aside and hold it with your hand covering the powder until the water is poured in.

Lesson: What a surprise it was for the people to receive a Savior, rather than a king.

Text: So they took branches of palm trees and went out to meet him, shouting, "Praise God! God bless him who comes in the name of the Lord! God bless the King of Israel!" [John 12:13; read John 12:12–19]

Outline

Introduce object: I'm thirsty. A nice glass of cold water sounds good.

1. Water is good. The people had reason to celebrate Jesus' accomplishments.

2. The flavored drink is even better. The people got more than they expected.

3. You can't understand how I did this? The people didn't understand what Jesus was doing either.

Conclusion: Wouldn't you like to go back in time to that joyful day and say to those people, "Are you in for a surprise!"

I'm thirsty. A nice glass of cold water sounds good. I like water. I'll pour myself a glass full (prepare to pour water into glass while you talk). The people who waved palm branches and shouted, "God bless the king!" were eager to praise and welcome Jesus because they had heard of the wonderful things he had done. Jesus' entry into Jerusalem was an exciting event.

(Pour water.) What's happening here? I'm getting something even better than I thought. This looks like lemonade. It tastes like lemonade. Now I like water, but I love lemonade. I'm getting something even better than I thought I would. The people cheering Jesus were about to get more than they ever expected. They were not getting a ruler for their land, a political ruler who would help them temporarily. They were getting a Savior for their lives and for eternity.

You can't understand how I did this? The people didn't understand what Jesus was doing either. They had their minds so set on receiving a king that they couldn't see something better—something more lasting! Palm Sunday is a day to celebrate Jesus' triumphant ride into Jerusalem. We know what Jesus was going to do in the next few days. Wouldn't you like to go back in time to that joyful day and say to those people, "Are you in for a surprise!"

27

Ouch!

(Good Friday)

Objects: A hammer, nail, and board

Lesson: Jesus died for you.

Text: They crucified him and then divided his clothes among them by throwing dice. After that they sat there and watched him. [Matt. 27:35–36]

Outline

Introduce objects: I need a volunteer to help me with this hammer and nail.

1. The soldiers pounded nails through Jesus' hands.

2. They watched him die.

3. Jesus was willing to die!

Conclusion: He did it for you.

I need a volunteer to help me with this hammer and nail. Have you ever hit your finger when you were pounding a nail into a board? It really hurts. Nobody does this on purpose, right? I'm going to ask my volunteer to do the pounding (hand the volunteer the hammer, then place your hand on the board and point the nail into the flesh on the top of your hand). Now would you pound this nail into the board?

I know, the thought of pounding a nail through my hand sounds terrible. How would you like me to do it to you? That is exactly what the soldiers did to Jesus. That was the way he died for us—by being nailed to a cross and hanging there.

If you got a nail through your hand accidentally, I'm sure you would rush to the emergency room at the hospital. You could have permanent, serious damage. Your hand would bleed all over everything and throb with pain. Do you know what the soldiers did when Jesus' hands were nailed to the cross? They sat there and *watched* him suffer. It was a painful and humiliating way to die. Yet he did it for you.

I'm glad you wouldn't pound this nail through my hand. I don't think I'm brave enough to let you do it. I don't know how Jesus ever could willingly be crucified. But he was. He knew it would be terrible and that he could get out of it—he was God, after all! But he did it anyway! He did it for you.

28

An Easter Lily

(Easter)

Object: An Easter lily

Lesson: The symbolism of the Easter lily helps us appreciate the true meaning of Easter.

Text: So they left the tomb in a hurry, afraid and yet filled with joy, and ran to tell his disciples. [Matt. 28:8]

Outline

Introduce object: The Easter lily is such a beautiful flower.

1. A lily has six petals, one for each of the letters in the word *Easter*.

2. The lily grows from a brown bulb, which shrivels as the plant grows. Our old selves "shrivel" as we grow as Christians.

3. The lily has a trumpet-shaped flower. We must herald the message of Easter.

4. The lily is white for purity. We are cleansed from our sins.

Conclusion: We are more than silent trumpets. Let us raise our voices in joy and thanks and praise. Happy Easter!

The Easter lily is such a beautiful flower. It has six petals—one for each of the letters in the word *Easter*. It is symbolic of Easter in many ways.

The lily grows from a bulb, a brown lump that shrivels as the flower grows. Our complete, fulfilled growth as Christians also depends on the "shriveling" of our old selves as we grow into the beautiful persons God wants us to be.

The flower of a lily is shaped like the bell of a trumpet to sound forth the joyful message: Jesus is risen from the grave! The lilies stand ready to herald the tribute if our voices fail or fade. Will our voices ring?

The lily is white—a clean, soft white for purity. Because of Jesus' death and resurrection we stand, like the lilies, clean and new before God with a bright and shining promise for the future.

The lily is symbolic of many things. We are more than symbols. We are God's true, live messengers in this world. We are more than silent trumpets. Let us raise our voices in joy and thanks and praise. Happy Easter!

Making an Easter Lily

Trace the pattern onto a sheet of white paper; cut.
Role paper in a cone shape.
Tape or paste the tab.
Roll the petals back on a pencil so they will curve outward.
Insert thin curved yellow strips of paper for stamens.
Glue on a pipe-cleaner stem.

The finished lily will look like this:

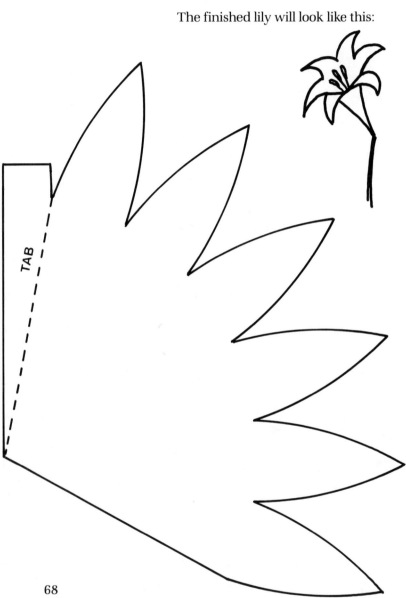

TAB

29

The Real Thing

(Easter)

Object: An imitation of a valuable object (jewelry, china, crystal, fur; I used an imitation Delft bowl)

Lesson: Faith is the real thing.

Text: "He is not here; he has been raised, just as he said. Come here and see the place where he was lying." [Matt. 28:6]

Outline

Introduce object: If this bowl had really been made in the original Delft china factory in Holland, it would be very valuable.

1. Many times in life we have to settle for second best and it is not important.

2. With our faith we can't afford not to have the real thing.

3. Jesus is real.

Conclusion: Praise God!

If this bowl had really been made in the original Delft china factory in Holland, it would be very valuable. The craftsmen there use an old secret formula and hand paint each object.

All I could afford is this copy. It looks nice, but I know—and now you know—that it is not real or valuable.

There are many times in life when we have to settle for less than best. Sometimes it is not important—generic can be as good as the most expensive brand. Sometimes it is not even wise to have the best. If this bowl were real and something happened to it, I would be twice as upset—and pity the poor person who broke or chipped it. I would have to spend a lot of time and energy worrying about this bowl and protecting it. Most of the time I prefer not to be burdened by these kinds of worries.

With our faith, however, we can't afford not to have the real thing. Just going to church does not bring us true Christian joy or make us Christians. Calling ourselves Christian doesn't give the peace that comes from true trust. Coming from a Christian family alone doesn't give us real inner faith and strength. Faith is something we accept and act upon and believe in our innermost selves. Then it is real. Then it is valuable.

We can't afford not to realize what Jesus did for us. We have a real sovereign God. We have real forgiveness. We have a real savior. We have real peace and joy and life eternal. Praise God!

30

Empty!

(Easter)

Object: An empty bag that looks full (another bag or a cut-down bag placed on the inside gives the illusion of fullness)

Lesson: The empty tomb means life eternal.

Text: They found the stone rolled away from the entrance to the tomb, so they went in; but they did not find the body of the Lord Jesus. [Luke 24:2–3]

Outline

Introduce object: Early in the morning, before the sun was up, the women carried their supplies to the tomb.

1. The women carried materials to wrap Jesus' body.

2. They found the tomb empty.

Conclusion: The women were only just beginning to understand and so their joy was tempered with fear. We do understand and so our joy is enriched with thanks and praise and gratitude.

Early in the morning, before the sun was up, the women carried their supplies to the tomb. (Carry bag as if it is heavy).

They wanted to wrap Jesus in cloths and preservatives, as was the custom of the time—not a very pleasant chore, especially since Jesus was to have been the king of the Jews and was to have rescued them from Roman rule. He was only thirty-three years old and he was very special. And now he was dead. The women came anyway. They wanted Jesus' body to be treated with respect. They had admired him while he lived.

But wait! When the women got there the tomb was empty—just as this bag is empty (turn over bag and shake). They didn't need their supplies because Jesus had risen—he was gone. They were very frightened, thinking that someone had stolen the body. But then the angel told them that Jesus had indeed risen from the dead, just as he said he would, and that they should go and tell this good news to the others.

The women were only just beginning to understand and so their joy was tempered with fear. We do understand and so our joy is enriched with thanks and praise and gratitude.

31

A Closer Look
at a Good Old Egg

(Easter)

Objects: A colored egg and a hollow eggshell

Lesson: Easter is the beginning of our new life.

Text: "Don't be alarmed," he said. "I know you are looking
for Jesus of Nazareth, who was crucified. He is not
here—he has been raised! Look, here is the place where
he was placed." [Mark 16:6; read Mark 16:1–7]

Outline

Introduce object: The egg that we decorate for Easter is
symbolic in many ways.

1. An egg is the beginning of life.

2. An egg sustains life when it is used as food.

3. An empty egg is like the empty tomb.

4. Decorated eggs come in all colors on the outside but
   are the same on the inside.

5. We use the expressions *good egg* and *bad egg.*

6. The verb *to egg on* means to encourage someone.

Conclusion: Especially let the egg remind you to praise God
for your new life!

The egg that we decorate for Easter is symbolic in many ways. The most important thing about eggs is that they are the beginning of new life. Many animals lay eggs. From the fertilized egg is hatched a baby, which grows into an adult animal. Easter is our beginning. Jesus died for our sins and rose again, giving us a new, clean beginning.

Eggs are used as food by many people and animals. Eggs are a good source of protein, which sustains life. The victory Jesus won on the cross sustains us—it gives us life eternal.

Let me crack this egg open. You all know what is inside of an egg (crack the hollow egg. Act like it will make a mess). It's empty! The women who came to the tomb on Easter morning expected to find Jesus' body there, but they found the tomb empty—a much bigger surprise than this empty egg.

We decorate eggs in all kinds of colors and patterns and designs. It's fun. Does this make them different on the inside? No, they still contain the familiar egg white and egg yolk. This reminds us that however different people look on the outside, they are all flesh and blood, children of God, sensitive human beings on the inside.

A fresh egg is delicious. An old or spoiled egg is terrible. From this we get the expressions we use to describe people. We call a person a "good egg" or a "bad egg."

To egg someone on means to encourage him. I would like to egg you on to consider all of the things this little egg has to tell us. Especially let the egg remind you to praise God for your new life!

32

Invisible But Not Gone

(Ascension Day)

Objects: A blackboard and a wet sponge (or steaming water, so the children can see the vapor going into the air and feel the moisture)

Lesson: Jesus' physical form went away but his presence remains.

Text: After saying this, he was taken up to heaven as they watched him, and a cloud hid him from their sight. [Acts 1:9; read Acts 1:9–11]

Outline

Introduce object: I'm going to get this whole blackboard wet.

1. The water on the blackboard evaporates. Jesus left the earth in his physical form.

2. Even though the water is no longer visible, it is in the air. Jesus' presence is also with us in another form.

Conclusion: A body can be in only one place at a time. But Jesus can now be with all those who love him.

I'm going to get this whole blackboard wet. Look at how shiny and black it is. Wait a minute! What is happening to the water that I just put on the blackboard? It is disappearing! It is evaporating! You can see the blackboard get dry again.

A long time ago Jesus led his followers out of the city. He said good-by to them and went up into the sky until he was hidden from sight by a cloud. We call the day we remember this Ascension Day. It is the day Jesus left the earth in his physical form.

Does this mean Jesus is gone, that he is far away from us? The water from the blackboard has evaporated, but it has not just disappeared. The tiny drops of water have gone into the air. They have taken another form. So too Jesus has not vanished or gone away. His presence is all around us. He knows us, hears us, helps us, and loves us. His presence is strong and close and real and powerful. We can't see him but it is as if we could all reach out and touch him.

A body can be in only one place at a time. But Jesus can now be with all those who love him.

5-31-98

33

With the Right Combination You Get Action

(Pentecost)

Objects: White vinegar (about an inch in the bottom of a clear container) and a spoon full of baking soda. You may want to demonstrate this twice.

Lesson: You need to be willing to use the power of the Holy Spirit.

Text: "How do you do this? What power do you have or whose name did you use?" [Acts 4:7b]

Outline

Introduce objects: In this container is a clear liquid which looks like water. This powder in the spoon looks like sugar, salt, or flour.

1. You need the right ingredients (vinegar and baking soda; the Holy Spirit and your willingness).

2. The ingredients will not react until they are combined.

Conclusion: With that combination you really get action!

In this container is a clear liquid which looks like water. This powder in the spoon looks like sugar, salt, or flour. What do you think will happen when I put them together? Let's see! (Combine the ingredients and enjoy the reaction.)

Were you expecting that kind of a reaction? It happens if you have the right ingredients—vinegar and baking soda. An even bigger reaction occurs when you combine the power of God found in the Holy Spirit and your willingness to do what he wants. If you think this was fun, you should try that combination.

These ingredients didn't do anything until they were put together. The power of the Holy Spirit is available to us, but we can ignore it. We need to recognize the power and be willing to use it. Then God can accomplish great things through us. Yes, we need to combine the power of the Holy Spirit with our interest, attention, and intention to make a difference, to be part of a powerful reaction, to be useful to and used by God.

With that combination you really get action!

34

A Strong Wind

(Pentecost)

Object: A model or picture of a windmill

Lesson: The Holy Spirit is a gentle and powerful influence in our lives.

Text: Suddenly there was a noise from the sky which sounded like a strong wind blowing. [Acts 2:2a; also read Acts 1–4]

Outline

Introduce object: This is a model of a windmill. A real windmill may be several stories high and large enough for a family to live in.

1. The power of the Holy Spirit is as strong as the wind, which can turn a windmill.
2. The power of the Holy Spirit is as gentle as a quiet breeze or a stirring in our hearts.
3. The Holy Spirit is as constant and dependable as the air around us.

Conclusion: On this special day when we remember the coming of the Holy Spirit to the early church, let us promise ourselves to have the power of the Holy Spirit in our lives every day.

This is a model of a windmill. A real windmill may be several stories high and large enough for a family to live in. It also usually has several gears and a large grinding stone. That is why it is called a wind*mill*—because the stone is used to grind wheat into flour for baking.

Do you know what moves the big grinding stone? The wind moves the blades, which turn the gears leading to the grinding stone. The wind is strong enough to be the power source of the windmill.

There is a powerful force that moves in our lives as well. When the Holy Spirit came to the early church there was the sound of a strong wind blowing. The Holy Spirit is still the powerful force in our lives that gives us the strength to meet new challenges, to overcome obstacles, to face difficult situations.

The Holy Spirit is also as gentle as a quiet breeze or a stirring in our hearts. It is a prompting to do God's will. It is a feeling of peace, comfort, happiness, and rest.

Wind is moving air. Air is always around us. The Holy Spirit is always there for us. We need to recognize and use this constant source of power and comfort.

On this special day when we remember the coming of the Holy Spirit to the early church, let us promise ourselves to have the power of the Holy Spirit in our lives every day.

35
Blown Up
(Pentecost)

Objects: One or more unusually-shaped balloons

Lesson: The Holy Spirit helps shape our lives.

Text: But the Spirit produces love, joy, peace, patience, kindness, goodness, faithfulness, humility, and self-control. [Gal. 5:22–23a]

Outline

Introduce objects: Here are several interestingly-shaped balloons.

1. A balloon without air is limp and useless. Without the Holy Spirit our lives lack fullness.

2. You fill a balloon with the invisible power of air. We are filled with the Holy Spirit.

3. Balloons come in different shapes, sizes, and colors. We have different inner shapes.

Conclusion: Let the Holy Spirit help you develop your unique potential.

Here are several interestingly-shaped balloons. You say that they don't look like much to you? I guess they don't look too interesting yet. They're just hanging limp and floppy. You really can't see their unique shape. Do you ever feel limp, unfulfilled, useless, or bored?

What can I do to improve these balloons? Okay, I'll blow them up. The invisible power of air fills the balloons. Now you can see what neat balloons these are. We all have the potential for being "blown up into interesting shapes." The power that does this for us is the Holy Spirit. When you feel limp and unfulfilled, let the power of the Holy Spirit inflate you into rewarding and exciting fullness. It sure beats being flat and useless!

There are many different shapes and sizes and colors of balloons. The Holy Spirit produces many gifts: love, joy, peace, patience, kindness, goodness, faithfulness, humility, and self-control. He helps us do many things. He makes us unique people. We are not all alike. We were not meant to be.

Let the Holy Spirit help you develop your unique potential.

5 - 24 - 98

36

Growing

(Seasons—Spring)

Object: A lima bean. Soak the bean overnight, open it carefully, and show the small plant (or make a drawing of the plant).

Lesson: All Christians have the potential for a full Christian life, but they need to develop.

Text: But continue to grow in the grace and knowledge of our Lord and Savior Jesus Christ. To him be the glory, now and forever! Amen. [2 Peter 3:18]

Outline

Introduce object: Have you ever looked at the inside of a seed?

1. Seeds have small plants in them—the potential for a mature plant. Christians have the potential for mature Christian life.

2. Seeds need soil, sun, and water to grow. Christians need prayer, fellowship, and study to grow.

Conclusion: When we see the tiny plant in this seed and think about the potential we all have for full Christian lives, how can we help but praise God!

Have you ever looked at the inside of a seed? This lima bean is a large seed. When I open it carefully, you can see a tiny bean plant.

Every seed is the beginning of a plant. Some seeds, however, are too hard to open or too small to see. Every Christian also has within him the beginning of a mature and fulfilling Christian life—the potential to be thriving, active, "full-grown," successful, and happy. Christians are ready to become all that God wants them to be.

This little plant will not grow unless I put it in the soil and it gets plenty of sun and water. In order for Christians to grow, they need the soil of fellowship—the friendship and nurturing of other Christians. They must have, for sun, the warmth of God's love received through prayer and close daily contact with him. They also need frequent waterings of study to learn more and more of how to live an exciting Christian life. Christians must be careful not to get stalled at an immature stage but to keep learning and growing and developing into a fuller and more beautiful "plant."

When we see the tiny plant in this seed and think about the potential we all have for full Christian lives, how can we help but praise God!

37

We Reap What We Sow

(Seasons—Summer)

Objects: Common vegetables

Lesson: Treat others kindly.

Text: A person will reap exactly what he plants. [Gal. 6:7b]

Outline

Introduce objects: In the spring I planted seeds in the garden and now look what I have.

1. You harvest what you plant.

    a. Each kind of seed produces a specific kind of plant.

    b. People respond to you in the same way that you treat them.

2. Having a positive attitude makes you a positive person.

Conclusion: That's the kind of harvest we all want to reap.

In the spring I planted seeds in the garden and now look what I have. What do you think grew where I planted the cucumber seeds? That's right, cucumbers. What grew where I planted the radish seed? Radishes, of course. Is it possible to get lettuce where I planted carrots? No, you always reap just what you plant or sow.

This is true in our lives and in our dealings with others as well. When you "sow" cheerfulness by being cheerful to other people, you get a warm and friendly response. When you are unkind or thoughtless, you make people unhappy and they will respond in an unhappy way. An act of kindness brightens a person's day and provokes him to consider doing a kindness for someone else. It also makes you feel good.

When you are kind, thoughtful, and considerate as God wants you to be, you make your life and attitudes and thoughts happier. You become what you have been doing. You begin reaping in your own life. That's the kind of harvest we all want to reap.

38

Show Your True Colors

(Seasons—Fall)

Objects: Leaves showing various fall colors

Lesson: Trouble can make us show that our faith is true. We need to be careful in choosing our friends.

Text: Be glad about this, even though it may now be necessary for you to be sad for a while because of the many kinds of trials you suffer. Their purpose is to prove that your faith is genuine. [1 Peter 1:6–7a]

Outline

Introduce objects: I love fall leaves, so I brought a big bunch of them with me today.

1. When trees lose their chlorophyll, they show their true colors. What does it take to make you show your true colors?

2. What color tree would you choose to be? Choose your friends carefully, because their "colors" rub off on you.

Conclusion: These leaves have given me a lot to think about!

I love fall leaves, so I brought a big bunch of them with me today. When the leaves on trees are green, the trees all look pretty much alike to me at a distance. I have to get close enough to see the shape of the individual leaves to tell the difference. In the fall, however, when the green chlorophyll is gone and the true colors of the leaves show through, I can spot the red of the red maple and the brown of the oak from far away.

What does it take to make you show your true colors? Do you need something that is missing from your life—love or friendship? Does a frustrating situation make you turn red? Do you turn green with jealousy when others have more than you do? Do you become a yellow coward when the going gets tough? Does the color drain from you when you face a difficult problem, serious trouble, or persecution? Or are you the kind of Christian who faces up to problems, seeks God's help and comfort, stands up to persecution, and shows the colors of a true believer?

These fall leaves give me something else to think about. If you were a tree and could choose your own color, what would you choose? That may seem like a far-out question, but when you choose your friends you are doing something similar. You need to look at their true colors, because you will be known as a member of their group. Their "color" rubs off on you in that you begin to act like them, to do the things they enjoy, and to use their expressions when you talk. So look at their true colors. What are they really like? How do they act in different situations? What do they want from life? Do they share your ideals and interests? Do you want to be like them?

These leaves have given me a lot to think about!

39
Snowflakes
(Seasons—Winter)

Objects: White paper and scissors. Fold up the paper and cut out different-shaped small pieces. When it is opened the paper resembles a snowflake.

Lesson: God has made us each unique. We should enjoy our differences.

Text: Love one another warmly as Christian brothers, and be eager to show respect for one another. [Rom. 12:10]

Outline

Introduce object: It is fun to fold this paper, cut out little designs, and make a paper snowflake.

1. When we make paper snowflakes, each is different.

2. God gave us snowflakes—each one is different.

3. God made people different. We should not try to make them the same but should enjoy the differences.

Conclusion: Praise God for this gift to us!

It is fun to fold this paper, cut out little designs, and make a paper snowflake. I like this one. Do you think I can make another one exactly like it? As hard as I have tried to do this, they all look different.

God has given us real snowflakes and each one of them is different also. Are you aware that no two snowflakes are exactly alike? Imagine that—millions of different snowflakes in a single snowfall! That is a fascinating thing God has done for us!

God has not made people exactly alike either. Each person is unique and special. We look different; we act different; we experience different emotions and needs. We love God and relate to people in our own way. This adds beauty and interest to our world.

Sometimes we try to make people all think and act exactly the same—just as we might try to make the same snowflake again. It doesn't work. Every person needs to grow and develop his Christian life and personality according to the unique potential God gave him. God could have made us all look, act, think, and respond the same way, but he didn't. We need to enjoy our differences, think about what makes each other special, and love and relate to God and our fellow Christians in our own unique way. Praise God for this gift to us!

40

Out of the Nest

(Mother's Day)

Object: A bird's nest

Lesson: On this special day, honor the mother God gave you.

Text: "Respect your father and your mother, so that you may live a long time in the land that I am giving you." [Exod. 20:12]

Outline

Introduce object: Peter found this bird's nest.

1. Birds shove defective babies out of the nest. Mothers care for their children regardless of problems.

2. Birds only feed and protect their young. Mothers are nurses, housekeepers, cooks, chauffeurs, friends, counselors.

3. Birds fly off and become independent in a season. Mothers are forever.

Conclusion: It is a special day to honor and thank the mother God gave you.

Peter found this bird's nest. The mother bird was finished with it so it's my turn to use it. It will help remind us of some important things about our mothers.

Did you know that if a mother bird has a defective baby she will shove it out of the nest and not allow it to grow up? Pity many of us if human mothers did that! Our mothers care for us regardless of how many problems we have. They take care of us when we are hurt or sick. They love us when we do wrong things.

A mother bird is kept quite busy feeding her babies and protecting them. But that is all she does. Our mothers have to be nurses, teachers, housekeepers, cooks, chauffeurs, friends, and counselors. Life can get quite complicated and demanding for our mothers. It's a wonder they *don't* try to push us out of the nest.

Baby birds grow up fast. They are out of the nest in a season. They are independent and the mother is free from caring for them. Our mothers are forever. They still do things for us and worry about us even when we get older. They never stop caring for us.

Mothers are a treasure. This is a special day to stop and think of all your mother does for you. It is a special day to honor and thank the mother God gave you.

41

Coordinate

(Father's Day)

Object: Chopsticks

Lesson: A good father-child relationship takes coordination.

Text: A wise son makes his father proud of him. [Prov. 10:1b]

Outline

Introduce object: Have you ever tried to use chopsticks?

1. A chopstick won't work alone. It takes two for a relationship as well.

2. To use chopsticks you need to coordinate movements. A father and child need to work together for a harmonious relationship.

Conclusion: When you work together, with God's help you can have a good relationship.

Have you ever tried to use chopsticks? It's pretty tricky! I'm amazed at how easily some people can use them. Let me see if I can pick up a few things with these chopsticks.

You can't use just one chopstick. The ends are not pointed

so there is little you could lift by stabbing it. You need to use two. On this Father's Day we need to remind ourselves that it takes two to make a relationship. The relationship between you and your father is a very special thing.

The hardest part of using chopsticks is getting the two sticks to coordinate. One has to cooperate with the other and you need to do this with the five fingers of one hand. You have to get the two points to meet so that they can pick up and hold food long enough to get it to your mouth. So too you need to cooperate with your father. You must work together or the relationship becomes shaky. You need mutual respect and understanding for harmony.

It's a tough job being a father. It's a tough job being a kid. You need to work at having a good relationship. You can do it! When you work together, with God's help you can have a good relationship.

42

Walking Forward

(Graduation)

Object: A wind-up toy

Lesson: Graduation is not only an ending but also a beginning.

Text: The one thing I do, however, is to forget what is behind me and do my best to reach what is ahead. So I run straight toward the goal in order to win the prize, which is God's call through Christ Jesus to the life above. [Phil. 3:13b–14]

Outline

Introduce object: It's fun to play with wind-up toys, but I wouldn't want to be like one.

1. The toy needs to be wound up. We have inner motivation.

2. The toy walks aimlessly. We need to head for the goal.

3. The toy operates mechanically. We have feelings and sensitivities.

Conclusion: Life is a process of walking forward one step at a time. This graduation is one of those steps.

It's fun to play with wind-up toys, but I wouldn't want to be like one. Not being like one will help me tell you about graduation.

Graduation is the end of one activity but the beginning of the rest of your life. It is a time to reach forward, to take direction, and to move on.

This toy can't do anything on its own. It needs to be wound up to work. It has no inner motivation. We do! We can make our own decisions and work to achieve our goals.

When this toy is wound up, it stumbles around aimlessly. There is no purpose to its actions. We can and need to set goals and head for them—especially the goal of becoming all that God wants us to be, of becoming complete and happy Christians.

This toy operates mechanically. It can't think or feel. It has no sensitivity to those around it. It can't relate to other people or interact with them. Thank God we are not mechanical. We can think, feel, and love. We can also sympathize with, fellowship with, and care for others.

God has not made us like mechanical toys. He gave us independence. He gave us minds and wills of our own. He gave us life.

Life is a process of walking forward one step at a time. This graduation is one of those steps.